WORDWISE

Creative Puzzles to Enrich Vocabulary

D1551026

Grades 6–9

DICTIONARY

Written by Pamela Amick Klawitter
Illustrated by Beverly Armstrong

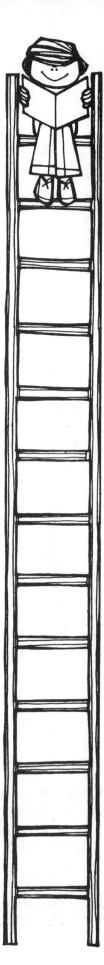

The Learning Works

Edited by Sherri M. Butterfield

The purchase of this book entitles the individual
classroom teacher to reproduce copies for use
in the classroom.

The reproduction of any part for an entire school
or school system or for commercial use is strictly
prohibited.

Copyright © 1990
The Learning Works, Inc.
Santa Barbara, California 93160
All rights reserved.
Printed in the United States of America.

Introduction

Wordwise is a clever collection of thirty-eight puzzles designed to challenge eager minds, develop vocabularies, and afford hours of old-fashioned fun. Based on the derivations, constructions, meanings, and sounds of words, these puzzles offer opportunities to explore compounds and anagrams, synonyms and antonyms, homophones and alliteration.

Puzzle workers are instructed to manipulate words in a variety of ways. For example, they are told to supply missing words and word parts, match words with their definitions, classify and categorize words, eliminate words from groups to which they do not belong, and use words correctly in sentences. In some instances, specific answers are called for. In other instances, the questions are more open-ended, and answers may vary. But in all instances, an answer key is provided.

Wordwise puzzles incorporate a vocabulary that ranges from *augur* to *xebec* and covers the globe from Antarctica and the Appalachians to Timbuktu and Zanzibar. These words are drawn from the fields of biology, geography, history, music, and more, and unexpectedly mix parts of the world with parts of speech. They include the familiar names of birds, fishes, and mammals, as well as the unfamiliar appellations of articles of clothing, musical instruments, and means of conveyance.

In short, its unique blend of skill-based activities makes **Wordwise** the ideal way to turn word work into word play.

Contents

Match Mates

All four words in each numbered group below can be meaningfully paired with a fifth word. Your task is to identify that fifth word and write it on the line. An example has been done for you.

Example: ___***house***___ bird   green   hold   plant
(bird**house**, green**house**, **house**hold, **house**plant)

1. _____   country   fire   road   word

2. _____   shot   skin   tooth   wheat

3. _____   club   gown   mare   time

4. _____   cast   letter   paper   print

5. _____   piano   slam   son   stand

6. _____   cuff   fry   horn   toast

7. _____   board   grown   hear   throw

8. _____   big   coat   dog   secret

9. _____   stand   water   wear   world

10. _____   style   throw   way   wheel

11. _____   act   first   high   room

12. _____   handle   hunt   kind   power

13. _____   boiled   die   ship   ware

14. _____   cup   fingers   fly   milk

15. _____   pack   pie   puddle   puppy

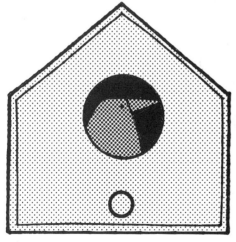 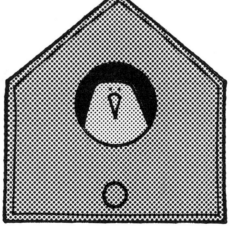 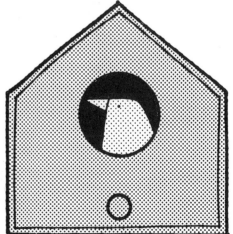

More Match Mates

All four words in each numbered group below can be meaningfully paired with a fifth word. Your task is to identify that fifth word and write it on the line. An example has been done for you.

Example: ___*end*___

book (book**end**)
dead (dead **end**)
table (**end** table)
zone (**end** zone)

1. _____
board
break
fit
strike

2. _____
back
boy
weight
work

3. _____
case
end
mark
note

4. _____
head
weight
house
street

5. _____
fine
finger
news
out

6. _____
hand
pack
stop
stroke

7. _____
ache
band
cold
first

8. _____
room
run
sick
work

9. _____
boat
jacket
size
time

10. _____
be
horn
range
shot

11. _____
chair
jump
light
rise

12. _____
lady
locked
mark
scape

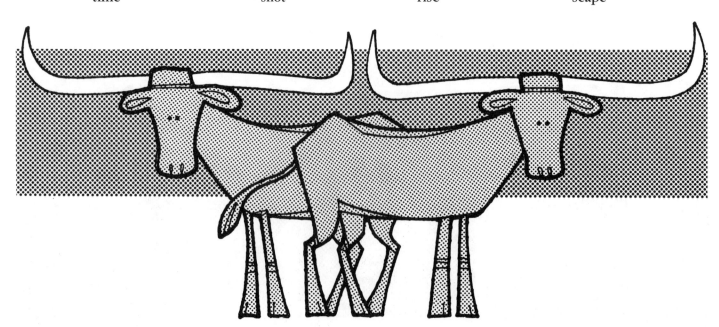

Letter Perfect

See if you can use the three letters on each numbered row to write three different words—one containing a total of four letters, one containing five to seven letters, and one containing eight letters or more. In all three of the words you write, the letters must appear in the order shown, but they need not occur consecutively. An example has been done for you.

Number of Letters

		four	five to seven	eight or more
Example:	gre	*ogre*	*glare*	*greenhouse*
1.	alm			
2.	bor			
3.	cal			
4.	cne			
5.	dot			
6.	eal			
7.	ern			
8.	fla			
9.	hme			
10.	lue			
11.	mnt			
12.	pag			
13.	sar			
14.	ste			
15.	tle			

sad sand salad salamander

Initial Investigation

Sarah wrote down the initials of every member of her class. Help her turn them into words. Use each numbered set of initials to write one or more words on the line beside it. The letters must remain in their original order, but they do not have to be used consecutively. An example has been done for you.

Example: SWT *swat,* *sweat,* *switch,* *sweater,* *stalwart*

1. AAA _____

2. BDG _____

3. BTM _____

4. CLN _____

5. DNT _____

6. GTR _____

7. LRN _____

8. MEA _____

9. OCR _____

10. PNC _____

11. PRA _____

12. RCD _____

13. STP _____

14. THT _____

15. WND _____

Members of the Same Group

Three of the four words in each numbered row name members of the same group. One word does not belong. Underline the word that does not belong and write the name of the group on the line. An example has been done for you.

Example: Arikara   <u>Madagascar</u>   Mandan   Modoc   ___***Indian tribes***___

1.	challis	chino	chintz	chitin	_____
2.	augur	ducat	franc	krone	_____
3.	sulky	umiak	xebec	yawl	_____
4.	clavier	lorry	sitar	tabor	_____
5.	canape	chalice	ewer	firkin	_____
6.	egret	macaque	petrel	rhea	_____
7.	bola	cudgel	kris	kudu	_____
8.	chateau	corbel	hogan	yurt	_____
9.	alewife	gar	okapi	tarpon	_____
10.	cassowary	euchre	pinochle	whist	_____
11.	brougham	gondola	landau	victoria	_____
12.	cholla	peyote	proboscis	saguaro	_____
13.	bamboo	bongo	fescue	millet	_____
14.	aphid	cicada	earwig	gavial	_____
15.	clavicle	gavotte	mazurka	quadrille	_____

Seeing Double

Each of these numbered terms contains a repeated syllable or word. Match these "seeing double" terms with their meanings by writing the correct letter on each line.

_____ 1. aye-aye

_____ 2. Bamm-Bamm

_____ 3. beriberi

_____ 4. bonbon

_____ 5. bulbul

_____ 6. cancan

_____ 7. caracara

_____ 8. dodo

_____ 9. fifty-fifty

_____ 10. hush-hush

_____ 11. Never-Never

_____ 12. Pago Pago

_____ 13. pawpaw

_____ 14. Sing Sing

_____ 15. so-so

_____ 16. tom-tom

_____ 17. tutu

_____ 18. twenty-twenty

_____ 19. Walla Walla

_____ 20. yo-yo

a. capital of American Samoa

b. dancer's skirt

c. resident of Bedrock

d. Persian songbird

e. imaginary land

f. hawk

g. soft-centered candy

h. perfect eyesight

i. disease

j. New York prison

k. city in Washington

l. stringed toy

m. French dance

n. confidential

o. fruit tree

p. shared equally

q. hand-beaten drum

r. neither very good nor very bad

s. tree-dwelling mammal

t. extinct flightless bird

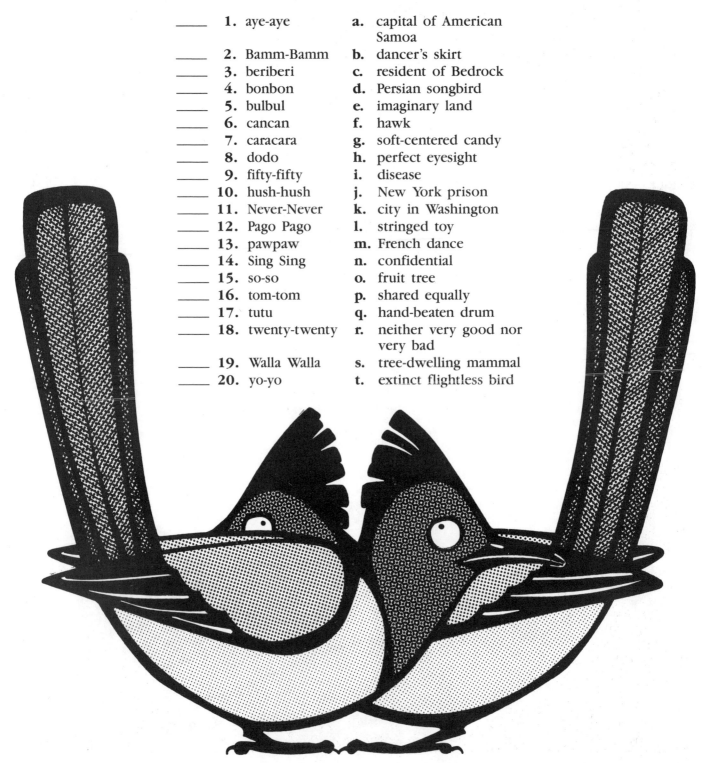

Spelling Stumpers

For each numbered definition below, a pair of words is listed. In each pair, both words are spelled correctly, but only one word matches the definition. Underline the word that matches. The first one has been done for you.

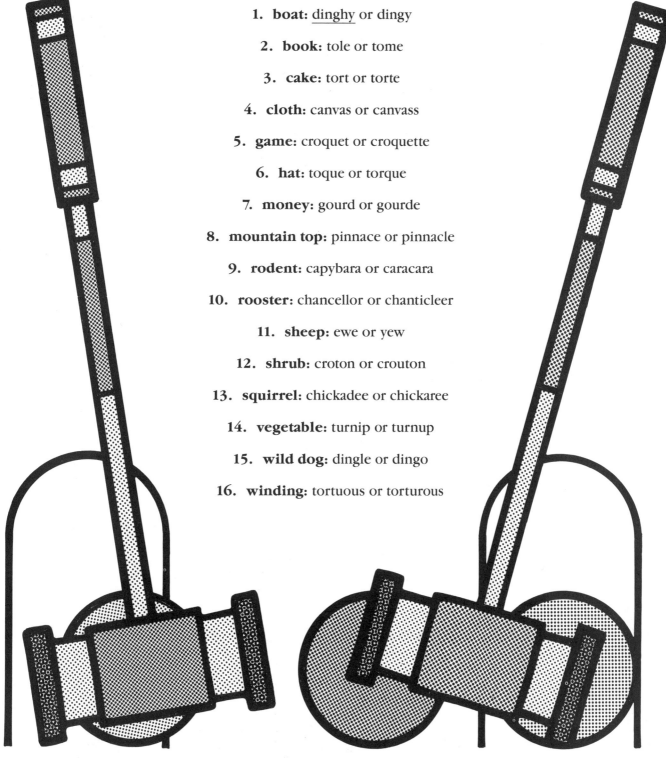

1. **boat:** <u>dinghy</u> or dingy

2. **book:** tole or tome

3. **cake:** tort or torte

4. **cloth:** canvas or canvass

5. **game:** croquet or croquette

6. **hat:** toque or torque

7. **money:** gourd or gourde

8. **mountain top:** pinnace or pinnacle

9. **rodent:** capybara or caracara

10. **rooster:** chancellor or chanticleer

11. **sheep:** ewe or yew

12. **shrub:** croton or crouton

13. **squirrel:** chickadee or chickaree

14. **vegetable:** turnip or turnup

15. **wild dog:** dingle or dingo

16. **winding:** tortuous or torturous

Homographs

Homographs are two or more words that are spelled the same but are different in derivation, meaning, pronunciation, or all three. Each numbered word below is one member of a homograph pair. It can be correctly pronounced in two different ways and has at least two different meanings. On the lines beside each word, write one sentence in which you use that word to reflect at least two of its meanings. Underline the word each time it appears.

Example: refuse   The landfill was forced to <u>refuse</u> the <u>refuse</u> because it was from another state.

1. address _____
   _____

2. collar _____
   _____

3. contest _____
   _____

4. convict _____
   _____

5. desert _____
   _____

6. excuse _____
   _____

7. object _____
   _____

8. present _____
   _____

9. record _____
   _____

10. reject _____
   _____

Anagrams

An **anagram** is a word or phrase created entirely by rearranging the letters of another word or phrase, without adding or subtracting any. For example, one anagram for the word *mantel* is *mental*. Another is *lament*. Write one anagram on the line beside each numbered word below.

1. dealer _____

2. garden _____

3. night _____

4. horse _____

5. react _____

6. rescue _____

7. scare _____

8. section _____

9. sever _____

10. slate _____

11. spread _____

12. stone _____

13. strap _____

14. stream _____

15. worth _____

BEETS

PEAS

Opposites Attract

Antonyms are words of opposite meaning. For example, the words ***build*** and ***raze*** are antonyms. The words in each numbered row below are an anagram for a pair of antonyms. Rearrange the letters in each row to form two new words that are opposite in meaning. Write the new words on the line. An example has been done for you.

Example: pace   ware   _____ ***peace*** _____ ***war*** _____

1. snow   lie   _____
2. pose   clone   _____
3. glare   malls   _____
4. sad   tints   _____
5. short   fad   _____
6. weld   on   _____
7. soft   laws   _____
8. dove   rerun   _____
9. dive   lie   _____
10. trots   past   _____
11. fund   stool   _____
12. wolf   miners   _____
13. lefty   plum   _____
14. shall   trot   _____
15. calf   pay inn   _____

To Be or Not Too Bee

Homophones are two or more words that are pronounced alike but are spelled differently and have different meanings. For example, the words **to**, **too**, and **two** are homophones. From the box below, choose the homophone pair that best completes each sentence. Then, write the correct member of that pair on each line.

1. The student _____ decided to _____ each student who broke school rules.

2. The bride walked down the petal-strewn _____ in the small church on the tropical _____.

3. Circumstances forced the architect to _____ his plans for the new church _____.

4. This morning's _____ of the newspaper contained an article about the new _____ to Central High School.

5. Harry's parents decided to _____ to his _____ of the mountain.

6. The school _____ is a person of _____.

7. The _____ of a skunk _____ the campers running in all directions.

8. The coach _____ his tug-of-war team to keep the rope _____.

9. The _____ of two hundred acres to the neighboring township was accomplished in a single _____ of the town council.

10. The council chairman will _____ the rule which says that the school must be built on a _____ that is within one-half mile of the town center.

Homophones

addition–edition	cite–site
aisle–isle	council–counsel
altar–alter	principal–principle
ascent–assent	scent–sent
cession–session	taught–taut

Tricky Trios

A **compound** is a word or term created by combining two or more words. For example, ***rowboat***, ***high school***, and ***devil-may-care*** are compounds. On each line below, write a word that can be combined with each of the adjacent words to form a compound. In several instances, you may be aware of more than one correct response, but you need write only one. An example has been done for you.

Example: black _____*mail*_____ box
(black**mail**, **mail**box)

1. about _____ lift
2. box _____ hat
3. bull _____ lash
4. busy _____ guard
5. butter _____ shake
6. cook _____ worm
7. deep _____ dry
8. double _____ stitch
9. eye _____ brush
10. fire _____ mat
11. first _____ room
12. hand _____ link
13. home _____ book
14. horse _____ horn
15. key _____ walk

16. kid _____ kin
17. launch _____ lock
18. mouth _____ cloth
19. oat _____ time
20. over _____ iron
21. pass _____ hole
22. pea _____ cracker
23. pit _____ dog
24. pop _____ cob
25. rain _____ tie
26. roller _____ board
27. sweet _____ chip
28. text _____ mark
29. top _____ rack
30. watch _____ stand

Missing Links

For each numbered row, supply the missing links. On each line, write a word that can be combined with either adjacent word to form a compound. An example has been done for you.

Example: chain ____*saw*____ horse ____*back*____ pack ____*rat*____ trap
(chain**saw**,   **saw**horse,   horse**back**,   **back**pack,   pack **rat**,   **rat**trap)

1. outer _____ station _____ wheel _____ lift

2. over _____ out _____ man _____ punch

3. square _____ time _____ top _____ service

4. bubble _____ drop _____ standing _____ mate

5. skim _____ cow _____ friend _____ shape

6. copy _____ fish _____ up _____ angle

7. sun _____ pot _____ beef _____ knife

8. honey _____ line _____ in _____ walk

9. tender _____ note _____ end _____ spoon

10. boot _____ fire _____ chuck _____ train

Four-Letter Zoo

Only animals with four-letter names live in this unusual zoo. Can you sort them out? First, read the name and decide whether the animal is a **bird**, a **fish**, or a **mammal**. Then, write the name in the correct column below.

cavy	ibis	pika
char	kite	puma
chat	kiwi	rail
chub	knot	rhea
coho	kudu	ruff
coot	ling	scad
dace	lynx	sole
goby	mola	teal
hake	oryx	vole
ibex	paca	zebu

Birds	**Fishes**	**Mammals**
_____	_____	_____
_____	_____	_____
_____	_____	_____
_____	_____	_____
_____	_____	_____
_____	_____	_____
_____	_____	_____
_____	_____	_____
_____	_____	_____
_____	_____	_____
_____	_____	_____

Say What?

Read each one of these uncommon words and decide if you could **listen to it**, **ride in it**, or **wear it**. Then, write the word in the correct column below. If you are unfamiliar with some of the words, look them up.

balalaika	flageolet	samisen
biretta	glockenspiel	sampan
brougham	hansom	shako
busby	howdah	sitar
chasuble	jodhpurs	sousaphone
dhow	ketch	surplice
doublet	landau	tabor
euphonium	lorry	toque
fedora	marimba	xebec
fez	ocarina	yawl

Listen to It	**Ride in It**	**Wear It**

Thumbs Up or Thumbs Down

You are trying to find a job and have been given the following alphabetized list of adjectives for possible use in writing your résumé. First, find out what each adjective means. Then, place it in the **thumbs up** column if you believe that using it to describe yourself, your reputation, or your accomplishments would help you get the job. Place it in the **thumbs down** column if you believe that using it in this way would hinder you in your quest for employment.

abrasive	impeccable
acrimonious	impetuous
adroit	ingenious
amenable	lethargic
assiduous	mendacious
brusque	perspicacious
capricious	quixotic
crass	sagacious
eloquent	sapient
fastidious	truculent
fractious	veracious

Thumbs Up   **Thumbs Down**

_____   _____

_____   _____

_____   _____

_____   _____

_____   _____

_____   _____

_____   _____

_____   _____

_____   _____

_____   _____

_____   _____

Name _____

Animal Compounds

A **compound** is a word or term created by combining two or more words. For example, *bullwhip*, *duck soup*, and *goose-neck* are compounds. First, make each lettered item below into a compound by writing the name of an animal on the line. Then, match these "animal compounds" with their definitions by writing a letter on the line after each number.

1. ____ infatuation
2. ____ a straight, direct course
3. ____ a period of hot, sultry weather
4. ____ roughhousing
5. ____ an open-air sale of secondhand goods
6. ____ a fruitless search
7. ____ a tight embrace
8. ____ something that disrupts the works
9. ____ hairdo
10. ____ a short snooze
11. ____ a scuba diver
12. ____ shabby, worn
13. ____ a mounted cattle ranch hand
14. ____ an ambitious worker
15. ____ an unruly tuft of hair
16. ____ a handheld microphone and loudspeaker
17. ____ slow moving
18. ____ a type of sweater
19. ____ a narrow walkway
20. ____ a stupid person
21. ____ the center of a target
22. ____ someone who bears the blame for others
23. ____ an inferior hotel or rooming house
24. ____ a game played with looped string
25. ____ a soldier's ID

a. _____ man
b. _____ hug
c. _____ wrench
d. _____ horn
e. _____ love
f. _____ cradle
g. eager _____
h. _____ nap
i. _____ -paced
j. _____ neck
k. _____ line
l. _____ tail
m. _____ days
n. _____ play
o. wild-_____ chase
p. _____ brain
q. _____ -eared
r. _____ boy
s. _____ bag
t. _____ tags
u. _____ lick
v. _____ -eye
w. _____ walk
x. scape _____
y. _____ market

It's Right There in Black and White

A **compound** is a word or term created by combining two or more words. For example, **black art**, **black-and-blue**, and **whitefly** are compounds. Each compound in the column on the right is incomplete. It should contain either the word **black** or the word **white**. First, complete each compound by writing one of these words on the lettered line. Then, match these black-or-white compounds to their correct definitions by writing a letter on each numbered line.

1. ____ ironworker; farrier
2. ____ a long, tapering, braided whip
3. ____ illegal trade in goods or commodities
4. ____ of or relating to salaried employees
5. ____ an old man
6. ____ a period of darkness
7. ____ an object of little or no value
8. ____ a card game also called *twenty-one*
9. ____ sign of truce; token of surrender
10. ____ wave crest breaking into foam
11. ____ leukocyte
12. ____ a discreditable member of a respectable group
13. ____ extortion by threat of public exposure
14. ____ a disease caused by inhaling coal dust
15. ____ a dense whitish star
16. ____ to cover up an unpleasant truth
17. ____ an electronic device used to record data
18. ____ an American Indian confederacy
19. ____ to vote against
20. ____ a bituminous material used to surface play areas and parking lots
21. ____ a bad reputation
22. ____ a rude or unscrupulous person; scoundrel
23. ____ a form of plague epidemic during the fourteenth century
24. ____ the executive mansion
25. ____ a dark, hard, smooth writing surface

a. _____ out
b. _____ flag
c. _____ board
d. _____ cap
e. _____ smith
f. _____ wash
g. _____ top
h. _____ elephant
i. _____ lung
j. _____ mail
k. _____ market
l. _____ dwarf
m. _____ jack
n. _____ -collar
o. _____ feet
p. _____ snake
q. _____ sheep
r. _____ box
s. _____ Death
t. _____ cell
u. _____ beard
v. _____ ball
w. _____ eye
x. _____ House
y. _____ guard

Rainbow Express

The compounds in the column on the right are incomplete. Each one should contain the name of a color. First, complete these compounds by writing the name of a color on each lettered line. Then, match the completed compounds to their correct definitions by writing a letter on each numbered line.

1. ____ inherited wealth

2. ____ an unusual ability to make plants grow

3. ____ a main course offered at a special price in a restaurant

4. ____ a member of a noble or socially prominent family

5. ____ architectural plan

6. ____ Lucille Ball

7. ____ a type of wasp

8. ____ a legal tender note issued by the U.S. government; dollar bill

9. ____ marked by ceremonial courtesy

10. ____ knives, forks, and spoons

11. ____ a retailer of fresh vegetables and fruit

12. ____ dungarees

13. ____ a medium between two extremes; moderation

14. ____ vigorous; lusty

15. ____ a tall, slender, smooth-coated dog used for racing

16. ____ of special significance

17. ____ an inexperienced or unsophisticated person

18. ____ to shirk duty or responsibility; goof off

19. ____ glass enclosure for plants

20. ____ a college athlete who is kept out of varsity competition for a year to extend his eligibility to play

21. ____ bruised

22. ____ something that moves very fast

23. ____ an infectious disease marked by jaundice

24. ____ to correct or revise

25. ____ a stock issue of high investment quality

a. _____ brick

b. _____ jeans

c. _____ back

d. _____ grocer

e. _____ house

f. _____ spoon

g. _____ plate

h. _____ hound

i. _____ thumb

j. _____ -and- _____

k. _____ ware

l. _____ blood

m. _____ shirt

n. _____ head

o. _____ jacket

p. _____ -carpet

q. _____ -blooded

r. _____ print

s. _____ fever

t. _____ horn

u. _____ mean

v. _____ -pencil

w. _____ chip

x. _____ -letter

y. _____ streak

Three-Letter Puzzlers

Complete the words in each numbered group below by writing the same three-letter word on all five lines.

Example: fa __*the*__ r
      o __*the*__ r
      __*the*__ me
      __*the*__ n
      __*the*__ se

1. br _____
   c _____ y
   h _____ le
   p _____ a
   str _____

2. app _____
   _____ ly
   h _____ t
   sp _____
   y _____

3. b _____ ch
   b _____ d
   _____ ch
   _____ k
   st _____ ge

4. _____ hem
   ch _____
   fr _____ ic
   gi _____
   pl _____

5. aff _____
   ch _____
   d _____ y
   f _____ ly
   st _____

6. _____ d
   _____ pet
   _____ rot
   _____ ry
   s _____ e

7. e _____ h
   he _____ h
   p _____ y
   qu _____
   st _____

8. g _____ d
   h _____ ly
   p _____ ed
   sc _____
   t _____

9. cr _____ e
   gr _____
   h _____ er
   l _____ her
   wh _____

son **win** **ray** **can** **pie**
far **act** **ton** **ore** **eel**
ham **bee** **fed** **one** **ink**

Four-Letter Puzzlers

In each numbered group below, you can turn the letters into words by writing the same four-letter word on each line. Your task is to identify and insert these missing four-letter words.

1. s_____
   re_____
   _____able
   ex_____
   _____ion

2. c_____
   ar_____
   inte_____
   w_____le
   p_____o

3. _____t
   wel_____
   _____dy
   be_____
   _____dian

4. _____y
   a_____
   _____ner
   de_____
   _____ial

5. co_____
   to_____
   _____en
   for_____
   re_____

6. in_____
   ro_____
   stu_____
   _____ist
   _____al

7. s_____
   a_____
   _____er
   _____y
   uni_____

8. b_____
   t_____
   st_____
   _____y
   ter_____

9. st_____e
   ar_____e
   o_____e
   _____er
   st_____le

10. b_____
    c_____
    f_____
    _____er
    un_____

11. s_____
    sp_____
    po_____
    ma_____
    _____nse

12. b_____
    _____on
    un_____
    care_____
    fear_____

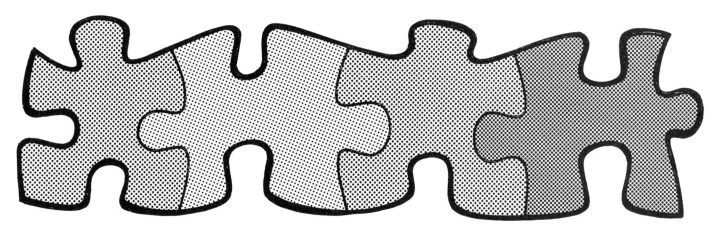

Don't Repeat Yourself!

For each numbered category, write at least six words in which no letter is repeated.
An example has been done for you.

Example: Body Parts *arm, ear, kidney, leg, lung, stomach*

1. Birds _____

2. Fishes _____

3. Flowers _____

4. Fruits _____

5. Insects _____

6. Mammals _____

7. Musical
   Instruments _____

8. Occupations _____

9. Sports _____

10. Tools _____

11. Toys _____

12. Trees _____

13. Vegetables _____

14. Vehicles _____

Candid Categories

Find two words to fit the fifteen categories listed down the left-hand side of the page and write each word in the appropriate column. To make your task more challenging, the words you write must have the number of letters specified and must be ones in which no letters are repeated.

Category	Number of Letters	
	One to Five	**Six or More**
1. A state in the United States	*Iowa*	*New York*
2. A city in the United States		
3. A river in the United States		
4. A president of the United States		
5. A country in South America		
6. A country in Africa		
7. A round object		
8. A man's first name		
9. A woman's first name		
10. A subject studied in school		
11. A two-syllable word		
12. A word with three vowels		
13. A verb		
14. An adjective		
15. Something found at the beach		

Hide and Seek

Find four ways to "hide" each three-letter word listed below in a longer word. The listed word can be hidden at the beginning, in the middle, or at the end of the longer word.

Example: **ham**

chamois

champion

hamburger

sham

1. ate

2. lip

3. oil

_____

_____

_____

_____

4. one

5. pea

6. rat

_____

_____

_____

_____

7. son

8. too

9. war

_____

_____

_____

_____

More Hide and Seek

Find four ways to "hide" each three-letter word listed below in a longer word. The listed word can be hidden at the beginning, in the middle, or at the end of the longer word.

Example: **ear**

earthquake

hearse

spear

1. are   **2. ash**   **3. her**

_____   _____   _____

_____   _____   _____

_____   _____   _____

_____   _____   _____

4. his   **5. man**   **6. ran**

_____   _____   _____

_____   _____   _____

_____   _____   _____

_____   _____   _____

7. rap   **8. tea**   **9. ton**

_____   _____   _____

_____   _____   _____

_____   _____   _____

_____   _____   _____

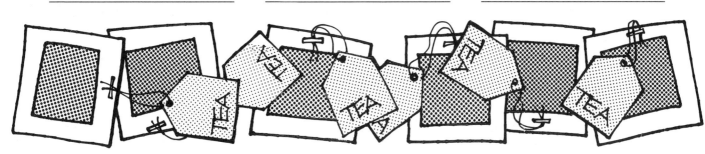

Synonym Search

Synonyms are words that have the same or similar meanings. In each numbered row, two of the three words are synonyms. First, underline the two synonyms. Then, find a more common synonym for this pair among the words in the box at the bottom of the page and write it on the line.

1. moniker   monocle   sobriquet   _____
2. indolent   slothful   energetic   _____
3. fallacious   veracious   specious   _____
4. retain   cede   relinquish   _____
5. docile   intractable   obstinate   _____
6. ductile   refractory   malleable   _____
7. accumulate   disperse   dissipate   _____
8. enmity   empathy   sympathy   _____
9. deleterious   innocuous   detrimental   _____
10. contiguous   isolated   conterminous   _____
11. exiguous   capacious   commodious   _____
12. malevolent   benevolent   malicious   _____

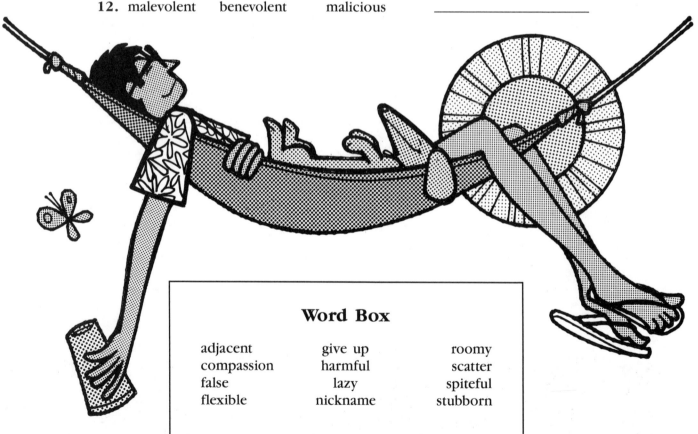

Word Box

adjacent	give up	roomy
compassion	harmful	scatter
false	lazy	spiteful
flexible	nickname	stubborn

Substitute Synonyms

Synonyms are words that have the same or similar meanings. Three of the words in each numbered row are synonyms. One word does not belong. First, read the words carefully. Next, underline the word that does not belong. Then, in the box at the bottom of the page, find a word that does belong. Finally, write this "substitute synonym" on the line.

1. munificent   niggardly   parsimonious   penurious   _____
2. chary   impetuous   prudent   vigilant   _____
3. depleted   stalwart   staunch   tenacious   _____
4. avarice   charity   cupidity   voraciousness _____
5. immotile   steadfast   stock-still   vivacious   _____
6. ambidextrous   pliant   refractory   versatile   _____
7. cantankerous   congenial   crotchety   irascible   _____
8. flaccid   irenic   pacific   placid   _____
9. jeopardous   perilous   scatheless   treacherous   _____
10. dulcet   raucous   stentorian   strident   _____
11. immaculate   squalid   taintless   unsullied   _____
12. annihilate   decimate   fabricate   raze   _____

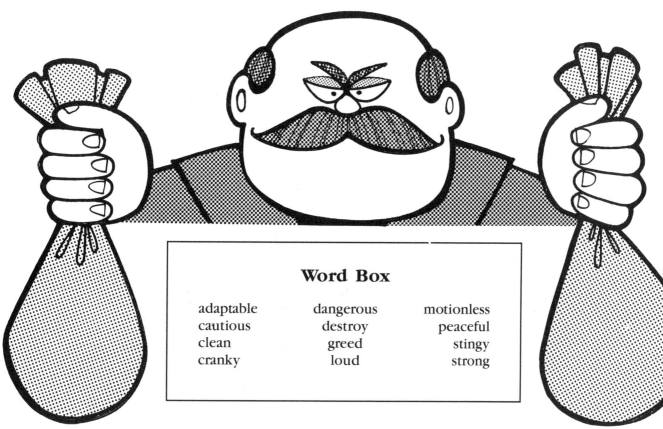

Word Box

adaptable	dangerous	motionless
cautious	destroy	peaceful
clean	greed	stingy
cranky	loud	strong

DO, RE, MI . . .

In solmization, *do*, *re*, *mi*, *fa*, *sol*, *la*, *ti*, and *do* are the syllables used to repre-
sent the eight tones of the diatonic scale. In the six numbered exercises below,
use these same letter combinations to create words of varying lengths by writing
one letter on each line. An example has been done for you.

Example: **D O**

      D O _T_

      D O _M_ _E_

      D O _I_ _N_ _G_

      D O _L_ _L_ _A_ _R_

      D O _O_ _R_ _M_ _A_ _T_

1. R E

   R E __

   R E __ __

   R E __ __ __

   R E __ __ __ __

   R E __ __ __ __ __

2. M I

   M I __

   M I __ __

   M I __ __ __

   M I __ __ __ __

   M I __ __ __ __ __

3. F A

   F A __

   F A __ __

   F A __ __ __

   F A __ __ __ __

   F A __ __ __ __ __

4. S O L

   S O L __

   S O L __ __

   S O L __ __ __

   S O L __ __ __ __

   S O L __ __ __ __ __

5. L A

   L A __

   L A __ __

   L A __ __ __

   L A __ __ __ __

   L A __ __ __ __ __

6. T I

   T I __

   T I __ __

   T I __ __ __

   T I __ __ __ __

   T I __ __ __ __ __

Word Pyramids

Complete each numbered word pyramid by writing letters in the open squares.
Caution: The words you create must be real words and must begin and end with the same letter.

1. D pyramid
2. G pyramid
3. M pyramid
4. N pyramid
5. S pyramid
6. T pyramid

Feline Fun

Each numbered word or phrase below defines or describes a word that happens to contain the smaller word *cat*. In each instance, write the *cat*-containing word. If you *cat*ch on and come through uns*cat*hed, reward yourself with a va*cat*ion!

1. butterfly larvae   c a t _ _ _ _ _ _ _ _

2. to capture   c a t _ _

3. to do away with   _ _ _ _ _ c a t _

4. to make an exact copy   _ _ _ _ _ c a t _

5. fragile   _ _ _ _ c a t _

6. group   c a t _ _ _ _ _

7. hard to understand   _ _ _ _ _ _ c a t _ _

8. the principal church of a district headed by a bishop   c a t _ _ _ _ _ _

9. livestock   c a t _ _ _

10. an olympic event   _ _ c a t _ _ _

11. to point out   _ _ _ _ c a t _

12. to provide food for an event   c a t _ _

13. a boat with twin hulls   c a t _ _ _ _ _ _

14. disconnected; abrupt   _ _ _ _ c a t _

15. to strew   _ c a t _ _ _

16. a seasoned tomato sauce   c a t _ _ _

17. a momentous tragic event   c a t _ _ _ _ _ _ _

18. underground passageways   c a t _ _ _ _ _ _

19. steep rapids; waterfall   c a t _ _ _ _ _

20. a book containing pictures and descriptions of articles that can be purchased by phone or mail order   c a t _ _ _ _

State Your Case

Each small word in the **States** box is contained in the longer name of a state. Each small word in the **Capitals** box is contained in the longer name of a state capital. Your task is to write the names of the twenty states and their capitals on the lines. Beware! You must use every small word once, and the states and capitals must match.

States			
car	hire	ode	set
cut	ill	on	sin
ego	lab	out	sip
for	land	rid	sour
gin	law	see	tuck

Capitals			
ale	go	over	ring
ash	hoe	pie	sale
cord	jacks	provide	see
cram	mad	rank	son
ford	nap	rich	ton

State

1. *Alabama*
2.
3.
4.
5.
6.
7.
8.
9.
10.
11.
12.
13.
14.
15.
16.
17.
18.
19.
20.

Capital

1. *Montgomery*
2.
3.
4.
5.
6.
7.
8.
9.
10.
11.
12.
13.
14.
15.
16.
17.
18.
19.
20.

Man, Oh, Man!

Match the **man** words in **Column A** with their definitions in **Column B** by writing a letter on the line in front of each number.

Column A	Column B
_____ 1. Managua	**a.** food miraculously supplied
_____ 2. Manama	**b.** the capital of Nicaragua
_____ 3. manatee	**c.** a grayish white hard brittle metal
_____ 4. mandamus	**d.** a stick-like insect whose forelimbs are held up as if in prayer
_____ 5. Mandan	**e.** a stringed instrument
_____ 6. Mandarin	**f.** the lower jaw
_____ 7. mandible	**g.** a public declaration of intentions or philosophy
_____ 8. mandolin	**h.** a yellowish red tropical fruit
_____ 9. mandrake	**i.** an American Indian tribe
_____ 10. mandrill	**j.** the primary northern dialect of Chinese used by the government and courts
_____ 11. maneuver	
_____ 12. manganese	**k.** large tubular pasta shells suitable for stuffing with cheese or meat
_____ 13. mango	**l.** a Mediterranean flowering herb
_____ 14. mangrove	**m.** a writ issued by a superior court commanding the performance of a specified act
_____ 15. manicotti	
_____ 16. manifesto	**n.** an aquatic herbivorous mammal
_____ 17. manna	**o.** an instrument used to measure the pressure of gases and vapors
_____ 18. manometer	**p.** a large fierce baboon
_____ 19. mantis	**q.** a strategic movement taken to gain a tactical advantage or end
_____ 20. manzanita	**r.** the capital of Bahrain
	s. North American evergreen shrub
	t. a tropical maritime tree or shrub that develops many prop roots and is important in coastal land building

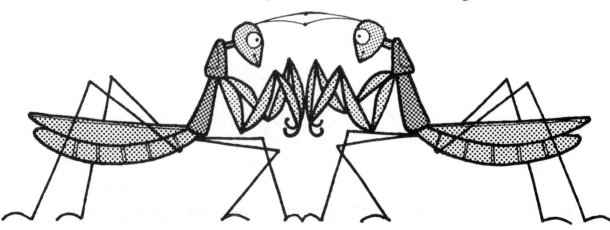

Category Search

Eight categories head the columns below. For each category, write words that begin with the letters listed down the left-hand side of the page. Several examples have been supplied.

	An Animal	A City	A Color	A Country
C	*cougar*	*Columbus*	*cerise*	*Canada*
A				
T				
E				
G				
O				
R				
Y				

	An Article of Clothing	An Adjective	A Word with 3 Vowels	A Word with 4 Syllables
S	*sari*	*sinister*	*special*	*spectrometer*
E				
A				
R				
C				
H				

Sentence Sense

Can you write a sentence in which there are at least six words and every word contains the same number of letters? Read the example and then try your luck using the numbers of letters indicated below.

Example: 3 letters _____ ***Six old men ate all the pie.*** _____

1. (3 letters) _____

_____

2. (3 letters) _____

_____

3. (3 letters) _____

_____

4. (4 letters) _____

_____

5. (4 letters) _____

_____

6. (5 letters) _____

_____

7. (6 letters) _____

_____

8. (7 letters) _____

_____

Slowly Stella Iguana surfed safely ashore.

A + Geography

Each numbered phrase describes a geographic feature. Using these phrases as clues, complete the names of the geographic features. *All* of the *As* are *a*lre*a*dy in pl*a*ce.

1. Mountain in Argentina which is the highest peak in the western hemisphere

   A _ _ _ _ a _ _ a

2. The smallest continent

   A _ _ _ _ a _ _ a

3. A province in Canada

   A _ _ _ _ _ a

4. A mountain in eastern Turkey near the border of Iran

   A _ a _ a _

5. City that is the capital of Jordan

   A _ _ a _

6. Country in southwestern Europe between France and Spain

   A _ _ _ _ _ a

7. Island off the coast of Venezuela

   A _ _ _ a

8. Desert in northern Chile

   A _ a _ a _ a

9. The largest continent

   A _ _ a

10. City that is the capital of Georgia

    A _ _ a _ _ a

11. Largest state among the United States

    A _ a _ _ a

12. City that is the capital of Maryland

    A _ _ a _ _ _ _ _

13. State whose capital is Little Rock

    A _ _ a _ _ a _

14. Canadian lake that lies on the border between Alberta and Saskatchewan

    A _ _ a _ a _ _ a

15. Ocean that separates North and South America from Europe and Africa

    A _ _ ·a _ _ _ _

16. The frozen continent

    A _ _ a _ _ _ _ _ a

17. The second largest country in South America

    A _ _ _ _ _ _ _ a

18. State whose capital is Montgomery

    A _ a _ a _ a

19. Country whose capital is Kabul

    A _ _ _ a _ _ _ _ a _

20. City that is the capital of Guam

    A _ a _ a

Double Vision Geography

Each geographic feature described below has a double vowel or a double conso-
nant in its name. Use the numbered clues and doubles to identify each one.

1. Country in northwestern Africa bordering the
   Atlantic Ocean and the Mediterranean sea

   _ _ _ _ c c _

2. The largest island in the Arctic archipelago

   _ _ f f _ _

3. Ancient Italian city destroyed in A.D. 79 by the
   eruption of Mount Vesuvius

   _ _ _ _ _ i i

4. City that is the capital of Wyoming

   _ _ _ _ _ n n _

5. City that is the capital of Burma

   _ _ _ _ o o _

6. Mountain system of eastern North America

   _ p p _ _ _ _ _ _ _

7. City that is the capital of West Bengal, India

   _ _ _ _ t t _

8. An island of Japan

   _ _ k k _ _ _ _

9. State that lies between Iowa and Indiana

   _ l l _ _ _ _ _

10. Group of islands admitted to the Union as the
    fiftieth state

    _ _ _ _ i i

11. River that is a tributary of the Missouri

    _ _ _ t t _

12. City that is the capital of Pennsylvania

    _ _ r r _ _ _ _ _

13. City in western Washington between Puget Sound
    and Lake Washington

    _ _ _ t t _ _

14. Country whose capital is Athens

    _ _ e e _ _

15. Former empire of Eastern Europe and northern
    Asia which is now the major part of the U.S.S.R.

    _ _ s s _ _

16. City in southeastern Wisconsin

    _ _ _ _ _ _ e e

17. City that is the capital of Manitoba, Canada

    _ _ n n _ _ _ _

18. Sea arm of the Atlantic Ocean bounded on the
    north and east by the West Indies, on the south
    by South America, and on the west by Central
    America

    _ _ _ _ b b _ _ _

Geography from A to Z

At least one letter of the alphabet is repeated in the names of these geographic features. Use the numbered clues to help you identify each feature, and write the missing letters on the line.

1. Desert region of southern Africa   __ **a** __ **a** __ **a** __ __

2. City that is the capital of Queensland, Australia   **B** __ __ __ **b** __ __ __

3. Northeastern state of which Hartford is the capital   **C** __ __ __ __ **c** __ __ **c** __ __

4. County in Florida   **D** __ **d** __

5. Swamp region in southern Florida   **E** __ **e** __ __ __ __ **e** __

6. City in north-central Arizona   **F** __ __ __ __ __ __ **f** **f**

7. Civil war battle site in Pennsylvania   **G** __ __ __ __ __ __ __ **g**

8. Largest Japanese island   **H** __ __ __ **h** __

9. Longest river in the United States   __ **i** __ __ **i** __ __ **i** __ __ **i**

10. City in northwestern Argentina   **J** __ **j** __ __

11. The Bluegrass State   **K** __ __ __ __ __ **k** __

12. City in northern Kentucky on the Ohio River   **L** __ __ __ __ __ __ **l** **l** __

(Geography from A to Z is continued on page 42.)

Geography from A to Z
(continued)

13. Nation that was formerly called Portuguese East Africa

M _ _ _ m _ _ _ _ _

14. Another name for Holland

N _ _ _ _ _ _ n _ _

15. River that flows through Venezuela

O _ _ _ o _ o

16. Group of islands for which Quezon City is the official capital

P _ _ _ _ p p _ _ _ _

17. City in central New Mexico

_ _ _ _ q _ _ _ q _ _

18. Highest mountain in the Cascade Range

R _ _ _ _ _ r

19. State of which Boston is the capital

_ _ s s _ _ _ _ s _ _ _ _

20. Famed city in Mali

T _ _ _ _ _ t _

21. Country in South America

U _ u _ u _ _

22. City in British Columbia

V _ _ _ _ _ v _ _

23. City that is the capital of Poland

W _ _ _ _ w

24. Chinese mountain near Nepal

X _ x _ _ _ _ _ _ _ _ _ _ _

25. Desert region in Russia

_ y _ y _ _ _ _

26. Island off the coast of Tanzania

Z _ _ z _ _ _ _

Name _____

The End

Each numbered word or phrase below is the definition of a word that happens to contain the smaller word *end*. In each instance, use the definition to complete the *end*-containing word. Sp*end* some time and do a spl*end*id job!

1. Saturday and Sunday   __ __ __ __ e n d

2. to make believe   __ __ __ __ e n d

3. buddy; pal   __ __ __ e n d

4. to give up   __ __ __ __ e n d __ __

5. to last   e n d __ __ __

6. mixer   __ __ e n d __ __

7. fashionable   __ __ e n d __

8. inclination   __ e n d __ __ __ __

9. thin   __ __ e n d __ __

10. to attempt   e n d __ __ __ __ __

11. to spread or stretch forth   __ __ __ e n d

12. eternal   e n d __ __ __ __

13. one who sells   __ e n d __ __

14. to expose to peril or place at risk   e n d __ __ __ __ __

15. huge   __ __ __ __ e n d __ __ __

16. protect   __ __ __ e n d

17. pay out   __ __ e n d

18. a guard over the wheel of a motor vehicle   __ e n d __ __

19. straps that pass over the shoulders and are used to hold up trousers   __ __ __ __ e n d __ __ __

20. an arrangement of time into days, weeks, months, and years   __ __ __ e n d __ __

Answer Key

Page 5, Match Mates
1. cross
2. buck
3. night
4. news
5. grand
6. french
7. over
8. top
9. under
10. free
11. class
12. man
13. hard
14. butter
15. mud

Page 6, More Match Mates
1. out
2. paper
3. book
4. light
5. print
6. back
7. head
8. home
9. life
10. long
11. high
12. land

Page 7, Letter Perfect
Answers will vary, but some possible responses are listed below.

1. palm — balmy — calamity
2. born — boring — elaborate
3. calm — scales — calendar
4. cane — cleaned — candelabra
5. dote — drought — doubtful
6. seal — healthy — earliest
7. tern — concern — southern
8. flat — foliage — conflagration
9. home — chimney — shameful
10. clue — blouse — cluttered
11. mint — amount — mountain
12. page — plague — champagne
13. sear — share — sparklers
14. stem — stencil — stethoscope
15. tile — title — startled

Page 8, Initial Investigation
Answers will vary, but some possible responses are listed below.

1. apparatus
2. building
3. Baltimore
4. clean
5. department
6. greater
7. learning
8. meadow
9. orchestra
10. picnic
11. prance
12. received
13. steep
14. thought
15. wind

Page 9, Members of the Same Group
1. Underline chitin; fabrics
2. Underline augur; coins
3. Underline sulky; boats
4. Underline lorry; musical instruments
5. Underline canape; containers
6. Underline macaque; birds
7. Underline kudu; weapons
8. Underline corbel; dwellings
9. Underline okapi; fishes
10. Underline cassowary; card games
11. Underline gondola; carriages
12. Underline proboscis; cacti
13. Underline bongo; grasses
14. Underline gavial; insects
15. Underline clavicle; dances

Page 10, Seeing Double
1. s
2. c
3. i
4. g
5. d
6. m
7. f
8. t
9. p
10. n
11. e
12. a
13. o
14. j
15. r
16. q
17. b
18. h
19. k
20. l

Page 11, Spelling Stumpers
1. dinghy
2. tome
3. torte
4. canvas
5. croquet
6. toque
7. gourde
8. pinnacle
9. capybara
10. chanticleer
11. ewe
12. croton
13. chickaree
14. turnip
15. dingo
16. tortuous

Page 12, Homographs
Answers will vary, but some possible responses are listed below.

1. The governor was forced to address a serious water shortage at the capitol, the state's most prestigious address.
2. The dogcatcher tried to collar the dog that was wearing a brown leather collar.
3. An unhappy participant decided to contest the rules of the contest.
4. Members of the jury were persuaded by the evidence to convict the former convict for a second time.
5. Mr. Smith was forced to desert his companions in the desert.
6. There is absolutely no excuse for asking the professor to excuse you from *three* class meetings!
7. The mayor did not object to spending the money when she discovered that the object of the search was a lost child.
8. The class chose Timmy to present the present to the teacher on her birthday.
9. "Just for the record, that is the worst record I have ever heard," declared the manager of the recording studio.
10. The line foreman's job is to make certain that the workers reject each reject at the inspection points.

Answer Key
(continued)

Page 13, Anagrams

1. leader
2. danger
3. thing
4. shore
5. crate
6. secure
7. acres
8. notices
9. verse
10. least
11. drapes
12. notes
13. parts
14. master
15. throw

Page 14, Opposites Attract

1. win–lose
2. open–close
3. small–large
4. stand–sit
5. soft–hard
6. old–new
7. fast–slow
8. over–under
9. live–die
10. start–stop
11. lost–found
12. smile–frown
13. empty–full
14. short–tall
15. plain–fancy

Page 15, To Be or Not Too Bee

The words should appear on the lines in this order.
1. council, counsel
2. aisle, isle
3. alter, altar
4. edition, addition
5. assent, ascent
6. principal, principle
7. scent, sent
8. taught, taut
9. cession, session
10. cite, site

Page 16, Tricky Trios

1. face
2. top
3. whip
4. body
5. milk
6. book
7. freeze
8. cross
9. tooth
10. place
11. class
12. cuff
13. work
14. shoe
15. board
16. nap
17. pad
18. wash
19. meal
20. cast
21. key
22. nut
23. bull
24. corn
25. bow
26. skate
27. potato
28. book
29. hat
30. band

Page 17, Missing Links

1. space — wagon — chair
2. look — door — hole
3. meal — table — secret
4. gum — out — room
5. milk — boy — ship
6. cat — hook — right
7. flower — roast — steak
8. bee — drive — side
9. foot — book — table
10. camp — wood — wagon

Page 18, Four-Letter Zoo

Birds	Fishes	Mammals
chat	char	cavy
coot	chub	ibex
ibis	coho	kudu
kite	dace	lynx
kiwi	goby	oryx
knot	hake	paca
rail	ling	pika
rhea	mola	puma
ruff	scad	vole
teal	sole	zebu

Page 19, Say What?

Listen to It	Ride in It	Wear It
balalaika	brougham	biretta
euphonium	dhow	busby
flageolet	hansom	chasuble
glockenspiel	howdah	doublet
marimba	ketch	fedora
ocarina	landau	fez
samisen	lorry	jodhpurs
sitar	sampan	shako
sousaphone	xebec	surplice
tabor	yawl	toque

Page 20, Thumbs Up or Thumbs Down

Thumbs Up	Thumbs Down
adroit	abrasive
amenable	acrimonious
assiduous	brusque
eloquent	capricious
fastidious	crass
impeccable	fractious
ingenious	impetuous
perspicacious	lethargic
sagacious	mendacious
sapient	quixotic
veracious	truculent

Page 21, Animal Compounds

1. e, puppy love
2. k, beeline
3. m, dog days
4. n, horseplay
5. y, flea market
6. o, wild-goose chase
7. b, bear hug
8. c, monkey wrench
9. l, ponytail
10. h, catnap
11. a, frogman
12. q, dog-eared
13. r, cowboy
14. g, eager beaver
15. u, cowlick
16. d, bullhorn
17. i, snail-paced
18. j, turtleneck
19. w, catwalk
20. p, birdbrain
21. v, bull's-eye
22. x, scapegoat
23. s, fleabag
24. f, cat's cradle
25. dog tags

Answer Key
(continued)

Page 22, It's Right There in Black and White

1. e, blacksmith
2. p, blacksnake
3. k, black market
4. n, white-collar
5. u, whitebeard
6. a, blackout
7. h, white elephant
8. m, blackjack
9. b, white flag
10. d, whitecap
11. t, white cell
12. q, black sheep
13. j, blackmail
14. i, black lung
15. l, white dwarf
16. f, whitewash
17. r, black box
18. o, Blackfeet
19. v, blackball
20. g, blacktop
21. w, black eye
22. y, blackguard
23. s, Black Death
24. x, White House
25. c, blackboard

Page 23, Rainbow Express

1. f, silver spoon
2. i, green thumb
3. g, blue plate
4. l, blue blood
5. r, blueprint
6. n, redhead
7. o, yellow jacket
8. c, greenback
9. p, red-carpet
10. k, silverware
11. d, greengrocer
12. b, blue jeans
13. u, golden mean
14. q, red-blooded
15. h, greyhound
16. x, red-letter
17. t, greenhorn
18. a, goldbrick
19. e, greenhouse
20. m, redshirt
21. j, black-and-blue
22. y, blue streak
23. s, yellow fever
24. v, red-pencil
25. w, blue chip

Page 24, Three-Letter Puzzlers

1. and
2. ear
3. ran
4. ant
5. air
6. car
7. art
8. our
9. eat

Page 25, Four-Letter Puzzlers

1. port
2. rest
3. come
4. part
5. ward
6. dent
7. corn
8. rain
9. rang
10. lock
11. lice
12. less

Page 26, Don't Repeat Yourself!

Answers will vary, but some possible responses are listed below.

1. **Birds:** blue jay, crow, heron, robin, swan, wren
2. **Fishes:** angelfish, catfish, halibut, marlin, pike, shark
3. **Flowers:** daisy, marigold, petunia, rose, sunflower, tulip
4. **Fruits:** fig, grape, orange, peach, pear, plum
5. **Insects:** dragonfly, housefly, ladybug, mantis, moth, wasp
6. **Mammals:** lion, monkey, sloth, tiger, whale, zebra
7. **Musical Instruments:** clarinet, drum, flute, guitar, piano, tuba
8. **Occupations:** dancer, editor, florist, lawyer, nurse, pilot, publisher
9. **Sports:** croquet, golf, hockey, rugby, skating, wrestling
10. **Tools:** ax, clamp, knife, saw, square, wrench
11. **Toys:** blocks, car, jacks, kite, marbles, top
12. **Trees:** ash, birch, elm, maple, pine, sequoia
13. **Vegetables:** beans, corn, okra, parsley, spinach, squash
14. **Vehicles:** boat, car, plane, train, truck, van

Page 27, Candid Categories

Answers will vary, but some possible responses are listed below.

	One to Five	*Six or More*
1.	Iowa	New York
2.	Salem	Mobile
3.	Snake	Hudson
4.	Ford	Garfield
5.	Peru	Brazil
6.	Egypt	Guinea
7.	tire	hubcap
8.	John	Albert
9.	Linda	Kirsten
10.	math	English
11.	many	blanket
12.	radio	coaster
13.	run	stumble
14.	ugly	solemn
15.	dune	bucket

Page 28, Hide and Seek

Answers will vary, but some possible responses are listed below.

1. *ate*: caterpillar, later, plate, statement
2. *lip*: clippers, flip, slipshod, tulip
3. *oil*: boiler, doily, soil, spoil
4. *one*: honest, money, stone, telephone
5. *pea*: appear, peanut, repeal, speak
6. *rat*: carat, crater, rather, ratio
7. *son*: bison, grandson, personal, sonata
8. *too*: cartoon, stool, tattoo, took
9. *war*: forward, toward, warden, wart

Answer Key
(continued)

Page 29, More Hide and Seek

Answers will vary, but some possible responses are listed below.

1. **are**: barefoot, careful, glare, share
2. **ash**: ashes, bashful, mashed, squash
3. **her**: catcher, father, herring, heron
4. **his**: chisel, hiss, history, thistle
5. **man**: command, foreman, managed, mantle
6. **ran**: brand, orange, rank, stranger
7. **rap**: drapes, rapid, therapy, wrap
8. **tea**: steal, teacup, team, tease
9. **ton**: baton, stone, tongs, tonic

Page 30, Synonym Search

1. moniker — sobriquet — nickname
2. indolent — slothful — lazy
3. fallacious — specious — false
4. cede — relinquish — give up
5. intractable — obstinate — stubborn
6. ductile — malleable — flexible
7. disperse — dissipate — scatter
8. empathy — sympathy — compassion
9. deleterious — detrimental — harmful
10. contiguous — conterminous — adjacent
11. capacious — commodious — roomy
12. malevolent — malicious — spiteful

Page 31, Substitute Synonyms

	Underlined Word	Substitute Synonym
1.	munificent	stingy
2.	impetuous	cautious
3.	depleted	strong
4.	charity	greed
5.	vivacious	motionless
6.	refractory	adaptable
7.	congenial	cranky
8.	flaccid	peaceful
9.	scatheless	dangerous
10.	dulcet	loud
11.	squalid	clean
12.	fabricate	destroy

Page 32, DO, RE, MI . . .

Answers will vary, but some possible responses are listed below.

1. red	2. mix	3. fan
reel	mind	fact
ready	misty	false
really	mingle	fasten
relaxed	mission	falling

4. solo	5. lap	6. tin
solar	last	time
solemn	laugh	tight
solvent	ladder	tickle
solitude	lashing	tigress

Page 33, Word Pyramids

1. **d**	2. **g**	3. **m**
dad	gag	mom
dead	gong	maim
dread	going	madam
depend	giving	museum
descend	growing	macadam

4. **n**	5. **s**	6. **t**
nun	sis	tot
neon	sons	taut
nylon	sixes	taunt
neuron	status	thirst
neutron	surplus	thought

Page 34, Feline Fun

1. caterpillars
2. catch
3. eradicate
4. duplicate
5. delicate
6. category
7. complicated
8. cathedral
9. cattle
10. decathlon
11. indicate
12. cater
13. catamaran
14. staccato
15. scatter
16. catsup
17. catastrophe
18. catacombs
19. cataract
20. catalog

Page 35, State Your Case

	State	Capital
1.	Alabama	Montgomery
2.	Arizona	Phoenix
3.	California	Sacramento
4.	Connecticut	Hartford
5.	Delaware	Dover
6.	Florida	Tallahassee
7.	Illinois	Springfield
8.	Kentucky	Frankfort
9.	Maryland	Annapolis
10.	Massachusetts	Boston
11.	Mississippi	Jackson
12.	Missouri	Jefferson City
13.	New Hampshire	Concord
14.	North Carolina	Raleigh
15.	Oregon	Salem
16.	Rhode Island	Providence
17.	South Dakota	Pierre
18.	Tennessee	Nashville
19.	Virginia	Richmond
20.	Wisconsin	Madison

Page 36, Man, Oh, Man!

1. b	6. j	11. q	16. g
2. r	7. f	12. c	17. a
3. n	8. e	13. h	18. o
4. m	9. l	14. t	19. d
5. i	10. p	15. k	20. s

Answer Key
(continued)

Page 37, Category Search

Answers will vary, but some possible responses are listed below.

	Animal	City	Color	Country
C	cougar	Columbus	cerise	Canada
A	alpaca	Atlanta	aqua	Argentina
T	tiger	Tallahassee	turquoise	Turkey
E	egret	Edinburgh	ecru	Egypt
G	gnu	Galveston	green	Guatemala
O	osprey	Omaha	orange	Oman
R	raccoon	Rio de Janeiro	red	Rumania
Y	yak	Yuma	yellow	Yugoslavia

	Clothing	Adjective	Word with 3 Vowels	Word with 4 Syllables
S	sari	sinister	special	spectrometer
E	evening gown	eerie	evening	eloquently
A	anklet	angry	accented	arbitrary
R	raincoat	rough	railing	relatively
C	caftan	cranky	crease	consequences
H	hose	heavy	heaven	hallelujah

Page 38, Sentence Sense

Answers will vary, but some possible responses are listed below.

1. *(3 letters)* The box top was all wet.
2. *(3 letters)* Sam saw the red hen eat.
3. *(3 letters)* The big dog cut his leg.
4. *(4 letters)* Five owls flew over that nest.
5. *(4 letters)* Four huge dogs will hide each bone.
6. *(5 letters)* Sarah plays piano after lunch today.
7. *(6 letters)* Elaine peeled twelve apples before dinner.
8. *(7 letters)* Fifteen friends finally arrived Tuesday evening.

Page 39, A+ Geography

1. Aconcagua
2. Australia
3. Alberta
4. Ararat
5. Amman
6. Andorra
7. Aruba
8. Atacama
9. Asia
10. Atlanta
11. Alaska
12. Annapolis
13. Arkansas
14. Athabasca
15. Atlantic
16. Antarctica
17. Argentina
18. Alabama
19. Afghanistan
20. Agana

Page 40, Double Vision Geography

1. Morocco
2. Baffin
3. Pompeii
4. Cheyenne
5. Rangoon
6. Appalachian
7. Calcutta
8. Hokkaido
9. Illinois
10. Hawaii
11. Platte
12. Harrisburg
13. Seattle
14. Greece
15. Russia
16. Milwaukee
17. Winnipeg
18. Caribbean

Pages 41–42, Geography from A to Z

1. Kalahari
2. Brisbane
3. Connecticut
4. Dade
5. Everglades
6. Flagstaff
7. Gettysburg
8. Honshu
9. Mississippi
10. Jujuy
11. Kentucky
12. Louisville
13. Mozambique
14. Netherlands
15. Orinoco
16. Philippines
17. Albuquerque
18. Rainier
19. Massachusetts
20. Timbuktu
21. Uruguay
22. Vancouver
23. Warsaw
24. Xixabangma Feng
25. Kyzyl Kum
26. Zanzibar

Page 43, The End

1. weekend
2. pretend
3. friend
4. surrender
5. endure
6. blender
7. trendy
8. tendency
9. slender
10. endeavor
11. extend
12. endless
13. vendor
14. endanger
15. tremendous
16. defend
17. spend
18. fender
19. suspenders
20. calendar

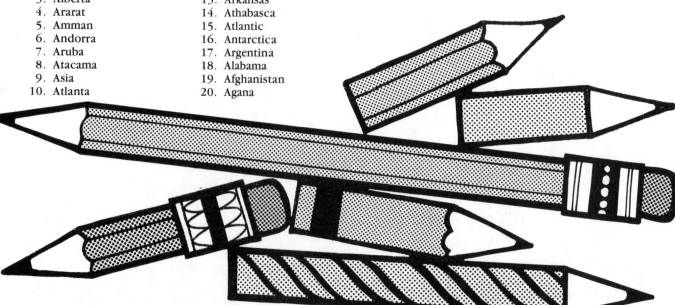